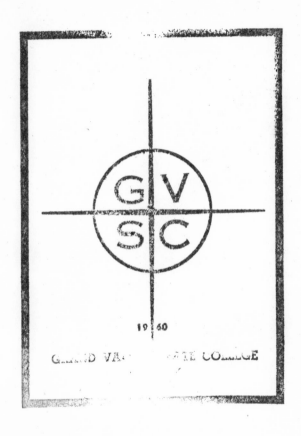

GVSC

19 60

GRAND VALLEY STATE COLLEGE

Bibliographical Series
of Supplements to 'British Book News'
on Writers and Their Work

*

GENERAL EDITOR
Bonamy Dobrée

¶ EDWARD GIBBON was born at Putney on 27 April 1737. He died in London on 17 January 1794.

EDWARD GIBBON

*from a painting by Henry Walton in the
National Portrait Gallery.*

EDWARD GIBBON

By C. V. WEDGWOOD

PUBLISHED FOR
THE BRITISH COUNCIL
and the NATIONAL BOOK LEAGUE
BY LONGMANS, GREEN & CO., LONDON, NEW YORK, TORONTO

LONGMANS, GREEN & CO. LTD.
6 & 7 Clifford Street, London W.1
Boston House, Strand Street, Cape Town
531 Little Collins Street, Melbourne

LONGMANS, GREEN & CO. INC.
55 Fifth Avenue, New York 3

LONGMANS, GREEN & CO.
20 Cranfield Road, Toronto 16

ORIENT LONGMANS LTD.
Calcutta Bombay Madras
Delhi Vijayawada Dacca

First published in September 1955

Printed in Great Britain at The Curwen Press, Plaistow, E.13

I

WHEN Edward Gibbon published the first volume of his *Decline and Fall of the Roman Empire* in 1776, it was hailed by the most eminent critics of his time as 'a truly classic work'. In the hundred and eighty years which have elapsed since then, that contemporary judgement has been confirmed. Gibbon's great book is still read for pleasure and information. The balance and lucidity of his presentation is as gratifying to the mind as a noble eighteenth-century building is to the eyes. The vigour of his narrative, the elegance of his prose and the sharpness of his irony still have power to enthrall and delight and, although seven generations of scholars have added to or modified our knowledge of the epoch, most of what Gibbon wrote is still valid as history.

Edward Gibbon was born at Putney, then a pretty suburban village a few miles from London, in the year 1737. His father was a gentleman of extravagant habits and comfortable means with interests in the City. In his youth he and his family had come under the influence of William Law and his two sisters are said to appear in Law's *Serious Call* as the frivolous Flavia and the devout Miranda. The devout Miss Gibbon continued to be Law's disciple and a pillar of his holy household until his death in 1761. It is strange that so close a link should exist between the great mystical writer and the highly rational historian.

As a child Edward Gibbon was small and sickly, easily bullied by tougher boys at Dr. Wooddeson's school where he was sent at nine years old to learn Latin. Of the seven children born to his parents he alone survived, and his delicate mother died when he was ten, when he was handed over to the care of her sister, Catherine Porten. Nothing more fortunate could have happened to him, for this excellent woman combined all the qualities most necessary to his health and happiness. She was resourceful, energetic, practical, deeply affectionate, imaginative in her understanding of his intellectual needs and not unduly possessive. To ensure herself an independent income and to make a more cheerful home for her nephew, she set up a little boarding-house in London for boys attending Westminster—the school which Gibbon himself attended on the rare occasions when he was well enough to do so. He gained his real education from the wide general reading in which she encouraged him. In the autobiography which he carefully composed in later life he called her 'the true mother of my mind as well as of my health' and left a grateful description of her personality: 'Her natural good sense was improved by the perusal of the best books in the English language and if her reason was sometimes clouded by prejudice, her sentiments were never disguised by hypocrisy or affectation. Her indulgent tenderness, the frankness of her temper, and my innate rising curiousity, soon removed all distance between us: like friends of an equal age we freely conversed on every topic, familiar or abstruse, and it was her delight and reward to observe the first shoots of my young ideas.'

In his twelfth year Gibbon describes himself as having fully developed that 'invincible love of reading, which I would not exchange for the treasures of India'. During the brief time that he was well enough to attend Dr. Wooddeson's school at Kingston he read Cornelius Nepos whose elegant simplicity he later commended as an excellent model. More important was his discovery of Homer in Pope's translation which, he says, 'accustomed my ear to the sound of poetic harmony'. In his mature style the influence of Pope's fluent precision in the use of words can still be traced. He read in the next two or three years everything on which he could lay hands—poetry, history, travel and romance—until in his own phrase his 'indiscriminate appetite subsided by degrees in the *historic* line'. He was fourteen when he came upon the *Universal History* while on a visit to friends and he 'was immersed in the passage of the Goths over the

Danube when the summons of the dinner bell reluctantly dragged me from my intellectual feast'.

When he was sixteen his health suddenly improved; the prostrating headaches from which he had suffered as a child vanished away and he was sent to the University to complete his education. Owing to his irregular schooling and wide but unconventional reading he arrived at Oxford in 1752 with 'a stock of erudition which might have puzzled a doctor and a degree of ignorance of which a schoolboy might have been ashamed'. But so slack was the tuition at Oxford at that time that no one took the least notice either of his erudition or of his ignorance. Teaching and discipline were equally lax and Gibbon, who was ardent to acquire knowledge, was bored and disgusted. Thrown back on his own resources during what he was later to call 'the most idle and unprofitable' months of his whole life, he began to examine the religious controversy recently caused by the publication of Middleton's *Free Enquiry into the Origin of Miracles*. The startling result of his researches into the early history of Christianity was his conversion to Catholicism, and he was privately received into the Church of Rome in June 1753.

As the law then stood in England, his conversion meant that he had to leave the University, and since Roman Catholics were excluded from public employment, it put a stop to any hope of a political or legal career. Gibbon's father, who was distressed at this unconventional turn in his son's life, packed him off to Lausanne to complete his studies and reconsider his religious views under the care of the Protestant pastor, Pavillard.

Gibbon stayed in Switzerland for nearly five years and there he laid the solid foundations of his education. His conversion had not gone deep; at Christmas 1754 he was reconciled to the Protestant religion. During the ensuing year he perfected himself in Latin and French, and formed the habit of writing his copious diaries entirely in French. He read French and Latin historians, began to learn Greek, toured

Switzerland and wrote for practice 'a very ample relation of my tour'. But his most valuable discovery was the important work on logic of the Abbé de Crousaz, which, he records 'formed my mind to a habit of thinking and reasoning I had no idea of before'. He now began to exercise his critical faculties by writing essays or, as he preferred to call them, 'observations' on Plautus and Virgil. He corresponded with neighbouring *savants*, saw the plays of Voltaire, and began to compose, in French, his *Essai sur l'Etude de la Littérature*. He knew that he wanted to be a man of learning and a writer, but he aimed at criticism or philosophy rather than history.

In June 1757 he met Suzanne Curchod, a pretty, intelligent, well-read young woman, the only child of a neighbouring pastor. Suzanne had no fortune except her intellect and her charms but she was greatly sought after. Gibbon's entry in his diary is short and telling:

> I saw Mademoiselle Curchod: Omnia vincit amor, et nos cedamus amori.

Gibbon himself was by no means unattractive. Although he was very small, his fresh colour and lively expression gave him charm and his conversation was fluent, witty and erudite; also he appeared to be a young man with a future. Mademoiselle Curchod, who had a good many admirers, was disposed to be coy. Gibbon pursued her. She held him off a little too long and by the time she decided to relent his own ardour was evidently cooling. But he could hardly admit that he had changed his mind, and when he left Switzerland in the spring of 1758, it was on the understanding that he would return to marry her. In his autobiography he gives a laconic and slightly disingenuous account of what next occurred. His father opposed the marriage and Gibbon, in his famous phrase, 'sighed as a lover but obeyed as a son'. He does not explain why, although he came home in May, he did not mention Suzanne to his father until

August, nor does he tell of Suzanne's desperate letters, imploring him to be true to her.

Gibbon was not made for domestic life and he probably knew it. He had the egoism of the natural scholar and wrote of himself 'I was never less alone than when by myself'. This is not the temperament that makes an ardent lover or a good husband. In a moment of youthful impulse he had thought himself in love with an intelligent young woman, but it is clear that his love evaporated when he began to think about the responsibilities and commitments of marriage. The sigh that he heaved as a lover, was a sigh of relief.

If Gibbon had the egoism very natural to scholars he had also an affectionate and grateful nature and his treatment of Suzanne is the only example of blamable personal conduct in his life. He was a good son although he had some cause for complaint of a father who never did much for him except squander his patrimony. The elder Mr. Gibbon had married again while his son was abroad; and it is much to Gibbon's credit that, although naturally apprehensive at first, he soon became devoted to his step-mother and remained so to the end of his life. In all the ordinary exchanges of family and friendship Gibbon was kind, reasonable, well-behaved and warm-hearted. But when it came to the stronger passions he failed, as scholars commonly do. Those whose first passion is knowledge justly fear the intrusion of any rival interest.

II

Gibbon was now twenty-one years old. He spoke and wrote French as fluently—at this time more fluently—than he did English. He had fully determined to devote his life to scholarship and writing though he had not yet settled on a subject. But for the next few years family interests and patriotic duty kept him in England. He had seen little of his father as a boy and nothing at all since he left Oxford. An excellent relationship now sprang up between the two, for the older Mr. Gibbon admired his son's erudition and enjoyed his company, and Hester Gibbon, the step-mother, who had no children of her own, was blessedly free from jealousy. In 1761 both father and son volunteered for the Hampshire militia. The Seven Years War was in progress and there were rumours of a possible French invasion. Nothing of the kind happened but Edward Gibbon spent the best part of two years marching about with the troops in Hampshire, living sometimes in billets and sometimes under canvas. Of this period he was later to say that 'the Captain of Hampshire grenadiers . . . has not been useless to the historian of the Roman Empire'. The part played by an English gentleman in local manoeuvres hardly seems on a level with the exploits of the great Roman generals and the ferocious barbarian leaders which Gibbon was later to describe. But the good historian should be able to use his own experience to illuminate that of others, and however absurd the comparison between eighteenth-century Hampshire and the battlefields of the fifth century must appear, however wide the difference between Captain Edward Gibbon of the militia and the thundering chiefs of the gothic hordes, there are certain unchanging elements in the soldier's experience which Gibbon learnt to appreciate.

He found much of the life very boring but he was young and strong enough to enjoy, in limited quantities, the rowdier amusements of his fellow officers. He did not however neglect his studies, went on steadily with his reading in all his leisure hours and completed the *Essai sur l'Etude de la Littérature* that he had begun at Lausanne. His proud father persuaded him to have this little work printed and when the King's brother, the Duke of York, came down to inspect the militia Captain Edward Gibbon, again to satisfy his father's whim, presented him with a copy. The Duke, sitting at breakfast in his tent, promised with conventional courtesy to read it as soon as he had time.

The little book is composed in elegant uninspired French,

imitated from Montesquieu. Gibbon himself, looking back on it from the eminence of his maturity, found it 'marred by a kind of obscurity and abruptness', confused and badly put together. It is indeed difficult to make out exactly what thesis Gibbon was trying to prove. 'A number of remarks and examples, historical, critical, philosophical, are heaped on each other without method or connection,' said Gibbon disparagingly, and the description is accurate. But the book contains one or two pages which reveal the writer's intelligence and his gift for history. In an admirable passage he compares Tacitus with Livy and praises the former as the ideal of the historian-philosopher. In another, he considers the nature of historical evidence and the framework of historical cause and effect within which all the other sciences are contained.

Irksome duty in the militia ended, with the war, in 1763 and Gibbon, now twenty-six years of age, set out on a second visit to the continent of Europe. He passed through Paris whence he wrote home that he had enjoyed better company and conversation in a fortnight than eighteen months in London could supply. Early in 1764 he was again in Lausanne and was certainly taken aback when he encountered Suzanne Curchod during an entertainment at Voltaire's house. The unhappy business ended not too graciously. The poor girl, who was now an orphan and very poor, still hoped to marry him. She wrote him long letters carefully, and intelligently, criticizing his *Essai sur l'Etude de la Littérature*. This was not perhaps the wisest way to win back a lover's heart but even had she used more feminine wiles, she would not have succeeded. Gibbon was determined to escape her and, covering the shabbiness of his own conduct by an easy self-deception, he convinced himself that she was a shallow and calculating flirt. 'Fille dangereuse et artificielle,' he wrote censoriously in his diary. Suzanne implored Jean Jacques Rousseau, then at Geneva, to see Gibbon and reason with him, but Rousseau replied that he liked nothing he had heard of Mr. Gibbon and thought him unworthy of her love. Suzanne gave up hope and shortly after married the elderly banker Necker.

She had done very well for herself and soon she was inviting Gibbon to her house to prove to him that she no longer loved him and that she had made a better match. The procedure was natural; it was also, as Gibbon did not fail to note in his diary, rather vulgar. But time smoothed away all asperities. In later years these uneasy lovers enjoyed a pleasant middle-aged friendship, and the elderly distinguished historian was once, to his amusement, the object of a proposal of marriage from Suzanne's precocious little daughter, the future Madame de Staël.

Gibbon was by no means exclusively occupied with Suzanne during his second visit to Lausanne. He renewed his friendship with the Swiss scholar, Deyverdun, who had been tutor to several distinguished young Englishmen including Lord Chesterfield's heir, and he made the acquaintance of another travelling compatriot, John Holroyd, later Lord Sheffield; these two were to be his closest friends for many years. Meanwhile he went on with his studies and accumulated voluminous notes on the ancient monuments of Italy in preparation for his journey there in a few months' time.

He was by now fairly sure that he intended to write history but his mind still wavered between a number of topics. He had considered a history of the Third Crusade, or of the Renaissance wars of France and Italy; or a life of Sir Walter Raleigh; or of the Marquis of Montrose; but by the summer of 1764 the principal subjects had reduced themselves to two. Either the Fall of the Roman Empire, or the Rise of the Swiss Republic.

About this time he visited the Court of Savoy, an occasion of which he has left a characteristically vivid description. He got on so well with the princesses of Savoy and 'grew so very free and easy that I drew out my snuff box, rapped it, took snuff twice (a crime never known before in the presence chamber) and continued my discourse in my usual attitude of my body bent forward and my forefinger stretched out'.

Gibbon was a young man of twenty-seven, with only an obscure pamphlet to his name, but he already had the confidence and the tricks of speech and gesture of a much older and more established scholar. What made Gibbon different from other conceited young men was that he had something more than great erudition and a lively talent for conversation; he had genius, as almost everyone was able to see.

There was another difference. In spite of his assurance, in spite of the vanity which sometimes made him ridiculous, Gibbon had the inner humility of the scholar in the face of his material. He was more eager to learn than to teach.

In the autumn of 1764 he left Lausanne for Italy and by October had reached Rome, whence he wrote, in what for Gibbon is almost a bemused strain, to his step-mother:

> I have already found such a fund of entertainment for a mind somewhat prepared for it by an acquaintance with the Romans, that I am really almost in a dream. Whatever ideas books may have given us of the greatness of that people, their accounts of the most flourishing state of Rome fall infinitely short of the picture of its ruins . . . I was this morning upon the top of Trajan's pillar. I shall not attempt a description of it. Only figure to yourself a column of a hundred and forty feet high of the purest white marble . . . wrought into bas reliefs with as much taste and delicacy as any chimney piece at Up Park.

The great conception already half formed in Gibbon's mind was taking shape, but he was able—and that is one of the attractive things about Gibbon—to remember that he was writing to a lady with no conception at all of what he was trying to describe; he brings it within the scope of her imagination, in the most natural way in the world, by comparing it to the carved chimney-pieces in a house she often visited.

Gibbon had thoroughly prepared himself for his visit to Rome by making careful notes of the topography of the classical city and the geography of Italy, and by mastering the science of medals which is of paramount importance in the study of Roman history. But his first experience was one of an unfamiliar and inspiring emotion which he has recorded in his autobiography.

> My temper is not very susceptible of enthusiasm, and the enthusiasm which I do not feel, I have ever scorned to affect. But at the distance of twenty five years, I can neither forget nor express the strong emotions which agitated my mind as I first approached and entered the eternal city. After a sleepless night, I trod, with a lofty step, the ruins of the Forum; each memorable spot where Romulus stood, or Tully spoke, or Caesar fell, was at once present to my eye; and several days of intoxication were lost or enjoyed before I could descend to a cool and minute investigation.

The crucial hour was now at hand and Gibbon has recorded it with due solemnity:

> It was at Rome, on the 15th of October, 1764, as I sat musing amidst the ruins of the Capitol, while the bare-footed friars were singing vespers in the Temple of Jupiter, that the idea of writing the decline and fall of the city first started to my mind.

Gibbon slightly dramatizes this great moment and it has been, perhaps pedantically, pointed out that his diaries show that the idea of writing something on the fall of Rome had been in his thoughts for some months before. But there is a considerable difference between the first foreshadowings of an idea and the moment at which a book takes shape and quickens within the author's mind. It is that moment which Gibbon, with his natural sense of the dramatic, has fixed and recorded.

But other interests still competed with the *Decline and Fall* and on his return to England in 1765 he turned once again from the vices of the Roman Empire to the virtues of the Swiss republic. He composed a long introductory section to a history of Switzerland, in French, and read it aloud to a literary society. By a rare stroke of good fortune, his listeners unanimously condemned it. 'The momentary sensation', writes Gibbon, 'was painful; but their condemnation was ratified by my cooler thoughts. I delivered my imperfect sheets to the flames and for ever after renounced a design in which some expense, much labour and more time had been so vainly consumed.' He had another reason for changing his mind. He did not know German and, although his friend Deyverdun was generously willing to help in this part of the research, he saw that to study the growth of the Swiss Confederation some personal knowledge of this 'barbarous gothic dialect' would be essential. About the same time, fortunately, he was persuaded to drop the curious vanity of writing in French.

So at last, about his thirtieth year, the stage was set for him to begin on his great book. He did not devote himself to it entirely but, in the intervals of his study, lived the easy social life of a cultivated gentleman, dining and conversing among the distinguished men of his time. He was for twelve years an almost entirely silent Member of Parliament and he held a minor government post as a Commissioner of Trade and Plantations, from which he derived a small additional income. This was welcome to him because his father, who had died in 1770, had not left him rich.

III

The first volume of the *Decline and Fall* appeared in 1776. It carried the story of the Roman Empire from the ordered tranquillity of the Antonine epoch through the intrigues, revolutions and disasters of the third century to the rehabilitation of the Empire under Diocletian and the establishment of Christianity as the official religion under Constantine: a hundred and fifty years of rapidly succeeding events and changing ideas. The opening paragraph of the great book immediately awakens interest, creates a remarkable and comprehensive picture of the age described, and reveals that air of learned and untroubled candour and that sure and shapely style which was to be maintained throughout the whole gigantic undertaking:

> In the second century of the Christian era, the Empire of Rome comprehended the fairest part of the earth, and the most civilized portion of mankind. The frontiers of that extensive monarchy were guarded by ancient renown and disciplined valour. The gentle but powerful influence of laws and manners had gradually cemented the union of the provinces. Their peaceful inhabitants enjoyed and abused the advantages of wealth and luxury. The image of a free constitution was preserved with decent reverence: the Roman senate appeared to possess the sovereign authority, and devolved on the emperors all the executive powers of government. During a happy period (A.D. 98–180) of more than fourscore years, the public administration was conducted by the virtue and abilities of Nerva, Trajan, Hadrian, and the two Antonines. It is the design of this, and of the two succeeding chapters, to describe the prosperous condition of their empire; and afterwards from the death of Marcus Antoninus, to deduce the most important circumstances of its decline and fall; a revolution which will ever be remembered, and is still felt by the nations of the earth.

Horace Walpole, prostrated by an attack of gout in the week of publication, sent round a note congratulating Gibbon on 'the style, manner, method, clearness and intelligence' of his first chapter and added, 'Mr. Walpole's impatience to proceed will give him such spirits that he flatters himself he shall owe part of his recovery to Mr. Gibbon'. A few days later he was writing to a friend:

> Lo, there is just appeared a truly classic work . . . The style is as smooth as a Flemish picture, and the muscles are concealed and only for natural uses, not exaggerated like Michaelangelo's to show the painter's skill in anatomy. The book is Mr. Gibbon's *Decline and Fall of the Roman Empire* . . . I know him a little, never suspected the extent of his talents for he is perfectly modest but I intend to know him a great deal more . . .

Walpole was wrong in imagining Gibbon to be modest, as he was later to discover. In every other respect his judgement has been fully confirmed by time.

The enthusiasm with which literary London received the book was not shared by the Anglican clergy. The first volume contained the famous Chapters XV and XVI devoted to the rise of Christianity and the treatment of Christians by the Roman Empire up to the time of Constantine the Great. It is a mistake to suppose that Gibbon was a militant anti-Christian; he was, rather, a typical product of the age of reason. He had acquired most of his philosophic ideas in the French-speaking part of Europe, and had come to accept the easy cynicism of contemporary French intellectuals as though it were universal. Their way of thought appealed naturally to his exact, unemotional mind. When he described his sub-ject as 'the triumph of barbarism and Christianity', when in his autobiography he slyly drew attention to the same thing in concrete form with his striking tableau of the ruins of the Capitol and the barefooted friars singing in the Temple of Jupiter, Gibbon was neither throwing out a challenge nor making propaganda against religion; he was stating what he felt to be the only accurate view of the matter. As the Church had gained in power, so Roman civilization had declined: that was a simple, inescapable fact.

The violent attacks which were soon made on his treat-ment of Christianity astonished and distressed him. 'I was startled', he writes, 'at the first discharge of ecclesiastical ordnance,' and well he might be for not only were angry pamphlets written against him but he was twice made the object of special attack in a sermon. Most of the criticism was as trivial as it was passionate, but one cleric, the youthful Dr. Davis of Balliol College, Oxford, accused him of mis-quoting his sources and plagiarizing other writers. These accusations Gibbon answered in a manner that exposed the presumption of his attacker. Gibbon was a thorough and careful scholar and he had a deep and comprehensive know-ledge of the available material. It is one of the minor ironies of history that he quarried so much of his book from the source materials laboriously assembled in the previous cen-tury by the great antiquarian and scholar Tillemont, himself a devout believer, who, in his pertinacious gathering of the documents, had certainly never intended them to serve the purposes of a writer with so different an outlook on the Church.

Gibbon's treatment of Christianity is in truth more offensive in manner than matter. Sainte-Beuve, whose analysis of Gibbon in *Causeries de Lundi* is particularly illuminating on this question, describes his writing as impregnated with a secret contempt for any feelings that he himself did not share. This contempt is all the more deadly for being cloaked in the guise of urbanity: as, for instance, in the famous paragraph in which he subtly discredits the initial miracles of Christianity.

> But how shall we excuse the supine inattention of the Pagan and philosophic world to those evidences which were presented by the hand of Omnipotence, not to their reason but to their senses? During the age of Christ, of his Apostles, and of their first disciples, the doctrine which they preached was confirmed by innumerable prodigies. The lame walked, the blind saw, the sick were healed, the dead were raised, daemons were expelled, and the laws of nature were frequently suspended for the benefit of the Church. But the sages of Greece and Rome turned aside from the awful spectacle, and, pursuing the ordinary occupations of life and study, appeared unconscious of any alterations in the moral or physical government of the world. Under the reign of Tiberius, the whole earth, or at least a celebrated province of the Roman Empire, was involved in a preternatural darkness of three hours. Even this miraculous event, which ought to have excited the wonder, the curiosity and the devotion of mankind, passed without notice in an age of science and history.

This attitude of ironical superiority towards believers still has the power to exasperate and provoke the devout. But Gibbon was not so much an anti-Christian as an agnostic. It was not religion that he disliked but exaggerated legends or meaningless rituals designed to captivate the multitude or make them amenable to the priest. Significant of this is his

famous dictum: 'The various modes of worship which pre-
vailed in the Roman world were all considered by the people
equally true, by the philosopher, equally false, and by the
magistrates, as equally useful.' This exact and careful state-
ment, relating to a particular epoch, is frequently misquoted,
and Gibbon is popularly credited with having said that 'All
religions seem to the people equally true, to the philosopher
equally false and to the magistrate equally useful'. Whether
or not Gibbon would have agreed to so general an assertion,
he did not make it. He was too good a historian to generalize
widely or wildly and his comments were usually in strict
relation to the epoch of which he was writing.

None the less his inability or unwillingness to sympathize
with an attitude of mind not his own is a blemish in his great
work. It closed his understanding to the irrational forces
which can inspire men to wisdom as well as folly. As the
fourth century, which principally occupies his first and
second volumes, was one of the most deeply and vehemently
religious epochs of European history, his blindness on this
point can be as irritating to the student of history as it is
offensive to the Christian.

The failing is part of Gibbon's character and outlook, that
very character and outlook which give to the whole history
its air of classic mastery. To wish Gibbon different is to wish
the masterpiece unmade, and even while we regret the
cynical pleasure which Gibbon evidently felt in demolishing
the miracles, and reducing the sufferings and the numbers of
the Christian martyrs in the Diocletianic persecution we
cannot but take pleasure in the sobriety of his argument and
the poise of his style:

> After the church had triumphed over all her enemies, the interest
> as well as the vanity of the captives prompted them to magnify the
> merit of their respective suffering. A convenient distance of time or
> place gave an ample scope to the progress of fiction; and the fre-
> quent instances which might be alleged of holy martyrs whose
> wounds had been instantly healed, whose strength had been re-
> newed, and whose lost members had been miraculously restored,

were extremely convenient for the purpose of removing every difficulty, and of silencing every objection. The most extravagant legends, as they conduced to the honour of the church, were applauded by the credulous multitude, countenanced by the power of the clergy, and attested by the suspicious evidence of ecclesiastical history.

Gibbon goes on to investigate the statistics of the glorious army of the martyrs and to suggest that, after all, only a small number 'sacrificed their lives for the important purpose of introducing Christianity into the world'.

The arguments in this passage are unexceptionable. But the tone implies not only an unwillingness to accept false martyrs and invented sacrifices but a disparagement of the emotions which inspired genuine martyrs to make real sacrifices.

This weakness in the book is also its greatness. It is Gibbon's capacity for writing of passionate and desperate times with a cool mind that enables him to write in general with such untroubled objectivity. It was not his gift to understand the hearts of men, but it was his duty and pleasure to understand their minds. He took great pains not only to read essential contemporary sources, but to be fully acquainted with the literature and the other productions of the ages he studied. If he did not understand the heart of a Christian slave he understood the mind of a Roman senator. If he did not greatly value the human passions he set the highest possible value on the human intellect. His own mind had developed in the favourable atmosphere of a time which delighted to call itself the Age of Reason. As one of his most acute modern critics, Mr. Christopher Dawson, has said, 'he stood on the summit of the Renaissance achievement and looked back over the waste of history to ancient Rome, as from one mountain top to another. The tragedy for him is the dethronement of a noble and intelligent civilization by force and ignorance. It is the triumph of the illiterate and the irrational that he records and deplores.'

While he understood the minds and the calculations of the

people about whom he wrote, he did not, like the romantic historians from Schiller onwards to Carlyle, throw himself into their hearts and try to share their feelings. The historic present—Carlyle's favourite tense—is practically unknown to Gibbonian grammar, a point of language which forcibly illustrates the change which the romantic movement wrought in the literary treatment of history.

But if Gibbon is not conventionally religious, neither is he indifferent to moral standards. He assumes that it is the right and duty of the historian to have a clearly defined moral attitude and he is exquisitely skilful in introducing judgement by way of implication. With what quiet contempt he deals for instance with the barbarian Ricimer, who, in the fifth century, elevated and destroyed puppet emperors at will. One of these, Majorian, was not only a man of strong and noble character but an old companion in arms. Majorian strove to revive the ancient discipline of the Romans; this did not suit Ricimer and he had to go. 'It was not perhaps without some regret', writes Gibbon, 'that Ricimer sacrificed his friend to the interest of his ambition.' In fifteen words he more perfectly exposes the baseness of Ricimer than he could have done in a paragraph of rhetoric. He carries on the story in the same tone:

> He resolved in a second choice to avoid the imprudent preference of superior virtue and merit. At his command the obsequious senate of Rome bestowed the Imperial title on Libius Severus, who ascended the throne of the West without emerging from the obscurity of a private condition. History has scarcely deigned to notice his birth, his elevation, his character or his death. Severus expired as soon as his life became inconvenient to his patron.

Gibbon's just and generous admiration is reserved for those who best display the classic virtues; justice, fortitude, perseverance, moderation. He greatly admires cleverness but never for itself alone. His morality, classical again in this, did not permit him to respect success unless it was allied with the virtues. He admires Diocletian, the hard-working self-made man who restored order to a distracted Empire more than Constantine who succeeded to his work and whose sly calculations and mercenary attitude to religion he found contemptible. He admires the men who failed nobly, like Julian the Apostate, or Majorian who strove to save the tottering fabric, and he despises those who succeeded ignobly.

IV

Gibbon's reputation was established by the publication of his first volume which ends with the triumph of Constantine. He was now something more than an erudite man and a good *raconteur*. He was an established historian equal in fame to Hume and Robertson, the two great figures whom he had admired in his youth. His vanity grew with his fame, or at least became more apparent, but since his erudition almost justified it and he had with it so much genuine good humour, his friends were disposed to regard it as an engaging foible. When he told an anecdote or illustrated an argument he liked to be listened to, and the gesture he has himself so well described—the body bent forward and the forefinger extended—was no doubt designed to attract the attention that it commanded. But he was not a conversation killer; he did not wish to hold forth all the time; he knew how to take part in a general discussion; and one of his younger friends, Lord Sheffield's daughter, was to leave it on record that he had a great gift for drawing out the opinions and ideas of the young people he met. This capacity argues a genuine interest in the ideas of others and a benevolence which counteracted the effects of his vanity.

But he did not like to be put out of countenance. Once at a dinner party he had told a good story and 'with his customary tap on the lid of his snuff box was looking round to receive our tribute of applause, when a deep toned but clear voice was heard from the bottom of the table very calmly and civilly impugning the correctness of the narrative'. Gibbon defended his position, but the deep-toned clear voice, which was that of the youngest guest present, would not be silenced. Seeing defeat imminent, Gibbon hurried from the table and was found by his host looking for his hat and cloak. 'That young gentleman', said Gibbon, 'is, I have no doubt, extremely ingenious and agreeable but I must acknowledge that his style of conversation is not exactly what I am accustomed to, so you must positively excuse me.'

The young gentleman, twenty-one at the time, was William Pitt, who would be Chancellor of the Exchequer at twenty-three, and Prime Minister at twenty-four. In later life he came to value Gibbon's company as Gibbon did his. Gibbon's vanity made him like the sensitive plant; he wilted for a moment at an aggressive touch but he soon recovered and retained no malice against his offender.

In 1779, four years after the publication of his first volume, Gibbon brought out the second volume, devoted to the invasions of the barbarians and the Circus quarrels at Constantinople. The subject was not so much to the liking of the polite society of the eighteenth century as that of the earlier volume, and Horace Walpole, who had so deeply admired the first, was disposed to be critical, objecting that so much time and skill should be spent on so unrewarding a theme. Gibbon was highly offended. He seems to have taken with much more humour the reception he got from the King's brother, the Duke of Gloucester, to whom he presented a copy. 'Another damned thick book?' exclaimed the affable prince. 'Always scribble, scribble, scribble, eh Mr. Gibbon?'

With the fall of Lord North's government Gibbon lost the small post on which he had depended for part of his income. He decided therefore that he would be able to live more peacefully and more cheaply in Lausanne, and by the autumn of 1783 he had transferred himself and his library to a delightful house which he planned to share with his old friend Deyverdun. The two scholars occupied separate parts of their pleasant mansion but met for dinner over which they discussed the problems and pleasures of their work, and entertained their friends from time to time. Lausanne society still abounded, as it had in Gibbon's youth, with intelligent and well-behaved ladies, and the two middle-aged scholars sometimes wistfully thought that a wife between them would not come amiss. 'Deyverdun and I have often agreed in jest and in earnest that a house like ours would be regulated, graced and enlivened by an agreeable female companion, but each of us seems desirous that his friend should sacrifice himself for the public good.' Each of them feared the obligations more than he valued the advantages of taking so momentous a step and they continued their bachelor existence. Gibbon knew how fortunate he was and wrote with a full sense of his blessings to Lady Sheffield describing his new library which commanded from 'three windows of plate glass, an unbounded prospect of many a league of vineyard, of fields, of wood, of lake and of mountains'. He concluded with satisfaction: 'An excellent house, a good table, a pleasant garden, are no contemptible ingredients in human happiness.'

Gibbon's admirable common sense and his freedom from any kind of self-deception, is one of his most attractive qualities. He did not want more than he had from life, and certainly by modern standards he had everything that a man could want. But comfortable means and ample leisure do not content everyone and many writers have been as happily circumstanced as Gibbon without being so contentedly aware of the fact or so grateful for their blessings. Gibbon was firmly and rightly contemptuous of the delusion, shared by many eighteenth-century intellectuals, that the ignorant peasant, free from the anxieties and speculations of the educated and powerful, was much to be envied. Frederick the Great was reported to have said to d'Alembert, as they walked in the gardens of Sans Souci, that a poor old woman, whom they saw asleep on a sunny bank was no doubt happier than they. 'The King and the philosopher may speak for themselves,' wrote Gibbon, 'for my part I do not envy the old woman.'

It was Gibbon's pleasant habit to work in a small pavilion at the end of his garden and here he finished the last volume of his great work, a moment commemorated in a famous passage in his autobiography. 'It was on the day, or rather the night, of the 27th June 1787, between the hours of eleven and twelve that I wrote the last lines of the last page in a summer house in my garden. After laying down my pen I took several turns in a *berceau* or covered walk of Acacias, which commands a prospect of the country, the lake, and the mountains. The air was temperate, the sky was serene the silver orb of the moon was reflected from the waters, and all Nature was silent. I will not dissemble the first emotions of joy on the recovery of freedom, and perhaps the establishment of my fame. But my pride was soon humbled, and a sober melancholy was spread over my mind by the idea that I had taken my everlasting leave of an old and agreeable companion, and that whatsoever might be the future date of my history, the life of the historian must be short and precarious.'

The quietude and peace of that scene is illuminating. Gibbon is a very great writer, and his book meant a great deal to him, but he never seems to have had—indeed it is unthinkable that he should have had—that intense relationship—love, hate, exasperation—that many great writers have with their work. His attitude to it is well behaved and under control like his writing: 'an old agreeable companion'.

The *Decline and Fall* itself ends with a deliberately low-toned passage. Sainte-Beuve, with his usual perspicacity, has said that Gibbon finishes 'cette longue carrière comme une promenade', and at the moment of setting down his pen pauses to consider the view and to take his ease. The closing paragraph describes the gradual unearthing of imperial Rome from the rubble of the Middle Ages. There is just a suggestion, but only a suggestion, of the new dawn, after the six volumes which have discussed the long decay and the final collapse of anything resembling or carrying on the tradition of the Roman Empire:

> Prostrate obelisks were raised from the ground, and erected in the most conspicuous places; of the eleven aqueducts of the Caesars and consuls, three were restored; the artificial rivers were conducted over a long series of old, or of new, arches, to discharge into marble basins a flood of salubrious and refreshing waters; and the spectator, impatient to ascend the steps of St. Peter's, is detained by a column of Egyptian granite, which rises between two lofty and perpetual fountains, to the height of one hundred and twenty feet. The map, the description, the monuments of ancient Rome, have been eluci-dated by the diligence of the antiquarian and the student; and the footsteps of heroes, the relics not of superstition, but of empire, are devoutly visited by a new race of pilgrims from the remote, and once savage, countries of the North.

That is the end of the book proper. Gibbon added a post-script, and after twenty years of work he could hardly have done less: he briefly summed up the story that he had tried to tell and concluded: 'It was among the ruins of the Capitol that I first conceived the idea of a work which has amused and exercised twenty years of my life, and which however inadequate to my own wishes I finally deliver to the curiousity and candour of the public.' To anyone acquainted with the sufferings and struggles of the writer, the exhilara-tions and frustrations and fallacious triumphs, or for that matter with the labours and problems of historical research, that phrase 'amused and exercised' must seem what perhaps it is—an understatement of Gibbon's activities in relation to his great book. Yet it may not be. The judicious use of exact but unexaggerated terms produces exact and unexaggerated reactions. Gibbon's style reflects and may also partly have shaped his character.

He came to England for the publication of his last three volumes, was given a splendid dinner by his publisher, attended the trial of Warren Hastings, and was made the object of a delicate compliment from Sheridan in his speech for the prosecution. 'Nothing equal in criminality is to be found', said Sheridan, 'either in ancient or modern history, in the correct periods of Tacitus or the luminous pages of Gibbon . . .' Later he teased Gibbon by asserting that he had said not 'luminous', but 'voluminous'.

V

It was now 1788, a year before the fall of the Bastille. The political storms in which the century was to end were on the point of breaking and literary fashions were moving fast away from the detached manner of Gibbon to the subjective and passionate manner of the romantics. In this year —1788—Schiller's play *Don Carlos* appeared as well as his passionate and vivid history of the Revolt of the Netherlands; Goethe's *Egmont* is of the same year. The turbulent reaction from the logic and order of French thought towards the exaltation of the passions and the ideal of a wild liberty was well on the way. Mirabeau, who had come to England shortly before the Revolution in search of radical inspiration in a country whose liberal institutions had been praised by Voltaire, looked about for English historians to translate into French. But for Gibbon, the greatest of them all, he felt only disapproval. At a large dinner party he fixed an indignant stare on a fat little man who had been pointed out to him as the author of the *Decline and Fall*, and spent the meal rehearsing what he would say to him. 'You, an Englishman!' he would say. 'No, you cannot be. You, who admire an empire of more than two hundred millions of men not one of whom could call himself free. You who extol an effeminate philosophy which sets greater value on luxury and pleasures than on virtue; you who write in a style which is always elegant but never vigorous—you are not an Englishman but at most a slave of the Elector of Hanover.' His courage, perhaps fortunately, failed him, for the object of his angry glaring was guiltless of the *Decline and Fall*. Gibbon was in Lausanne at the time.

Mirabeau's view is unfair; like many other critics of Gibbon, he had not read the book. What Gibbon admired in the Roman Empire was not its expanse and power, still less its authority over the individual. What he admired was the spectacle of peaceful order which enabled the arts of civilization to be practised. He did not admire effeminate philosophies and luxuries, and he deplored the decay of democratic institutions while appreciating the craft with which successive Emperors had curtailed them. His admiration was reserved for the strong classical virtues, for reason and restraint.

If the rising romantics, and the poor young *exaltés* of liberty who were soon to have such a rude awakening, found much to criticize in Gibbon's book, its reception among the discriminating older generation surpassed even the author's by no means modest hopes. Adam Smith pronounced him 'at the very head of the whole literary tribe at present existing in Europe'. He was generally acclaimed as the greatest of English historians—a position from which he has not yet been dethroned.

On his return to Lausanne after his triumph in London he found things were no longer what they had been. His friend Deyverdun was dead. The romantic movement had launched upon the country a quantity of staring tourists, come 'to view the glaciers'. Gibbon was also perturbed by the 'furious spirit of democracy' which had been let loose by the French Revolution. His own political views are best summed up in the comment which he made at this time on the internal politics of Switzerland. Lausanne, long unwillingly subjected to the aristocratic government of Bern, was stirring uneasily. Gibbon had no patience with this nonsense: 'While the aristocracy of Bern protects the happiness, it is superfluous to enquire whether it be founded on the rights of man,' he wrote.

Fascinated by the politics of the past, he was resentful of the politics of the present because they threatened his calm retreat. Lausanne was now full of refugees from the Revolution. 'These noble fugitives', he wrote, 'are entitled to our pity; they may claim our esteem, but they cannot, in their present state of mind and fortune, much contribute to our amusement. Instead of looking down as calm and idle spectators on the theatre of Europe, our domestic harmony is somewhat embittered by the infusion of party spirit.' The comment is curiously insensitive, and Gibbon's public comments are indeed often out of key with the natural kindliness he showed in his personal life.

In the summer of 1793 his great friend Lord Sheffield was suddenly left a widower. His wife, reacting very differently from Gibbon, had fallen ill owing to long and strenuous hours of work on behalf of homeless French refugees in England. Gibbon, genuinely distressed at his friend's grief, hurried home to console him. He passed the summer between London and Lord Sheffield's country-house and was able both to give comfort and to receive much pleasure from the company of Lord Sheffield's daughters and their young friends. He was only fifty-six and at the height of his intellectual power. A great edition of English mediaeval documents, of which he was to be the editor, was projected and he looked forward to the new work, declaring with confidence that he was good for ten or twelve more years of valuable work. But his friends had grown alarmed for the state of his health. His vanity prevented him from admitting that the hydrocele from which he was suffering had reached embarrassingly large proportions. At length, however, he agreed to an operation in the autumn of 1793. This was temporarily successful but the condition worsened again in January. Gibbon was now taking quinine every six hours and drinking five glasses of madeira at dinner on doctor's orders. In the circumstances it is not surprising that the immediate cause of his death, on 17 January 1794, appears to have been cirrhosis of the liver.

English history lost a remarkable piece of editing when Gibbon died before he could begin work on the documents. But anything after the *Decline and Fall* would have been an anti-climax. His life's work is the one massive, incomparable book, and all the rest that he left behind him is interesting chiefly for the light it throws on the mind and the method behind the great history. Lord Sheffield piously edited his autobiography, his occasional pieces, and some of his letters. In more recent years his journals and the earlier versions of the autobiography have been given to the world, with many more of his letters.

The *Decline and Fall* stands alone in English historical literature. Style and structure apart, its erudition still amazes; what other history has stood the test of seven generations of scholarship and criticism without being wholly superseded? Gibbon's views have been modified and added to; yet his book remains basically the standard work for the decline of Rome, at least, if not for the Byzantine empire.

Of the style and structure it is hard to speak briefly. His unique quality—unique, that is, among English narrative historians—is his exact control. Most English historians of any literary sensibility are given to passion; the quality is inherent in the calling. They become involved in the events they describe, are moved, excited, carried away. This makes for vigorous writing and sometimes for a sharper insight into character, but it does not make for a steady, comprehensive vision, or for clear presentation.

The English as writers have a false conception of themselves. We do not think of ourselves as passionate, yet the great strength and almost all the faults of English writing arise from passion. We are among the most passionate and impulsive writers in the modern world. We commonly set more value on something called 'sincerity'—a word which often describes what happens when a writer loses control of his material—than on symmetry and order. We are the first to condemn a deliberate and perfected work of art as 'dead'. Sometimes this judgement may be right, but often it is no

more than an angry prejudice arising from our own vehe-
ment and untidy minds. Consider for instance how few
Englishmen are really capable of appreciating the flawless
achievement of Racine. Shakespeare, the transcendant artist
who broke all the rules, has left to his countrymen an un-
written charter to despise regulations.

Gibbon was not entirely without passion, for his love of
learning and reverence for the intellect amount to passion.
But he kept it within bounds and when he wrote, his first
thought was for the whole work of art. Each sentence per-
forms its right function in relation to what goes before and
after, each paragraph carries the narrative on at the necessary
pace, or establishes a point in the exposition. Because of this
attention to detail the massive volumes are always easy to
read and never monotonous. The narrative passages are
never clogged with intensive exposition, and the expository
paragraphs and chapters stand out with a fine static clarity.
Gibbon's control of his material was so sure and his sense of
form so strong that he seems to have been able, at least in
his later volumes, to achieve his effects without rewriting.
His plan was clear in advance and he would write his sen-
tences in his head and commit them to paper only when he
was satisfied of their completeness. In earlier times, when he
still rewrote substantially, it seems to have been the form or
order of each chapter rather than the shape of each sentence
which gave him anxiety. Of his first volume he wrote to
Lord Sheffield: 'The first chapter has been composed *de
nouveau*, three times, the second twice' and he spoke of an
intention to '*refondre*' or recast other important parts of the
book.

Gibbon's style is highly cultivated and therefore arti-
ficial. It is also a dangerous style to copy and he has suffered
badly from imitators who aped his mannerisms without
understanding their purpose and without having the sensitive ear and varied vocabulary which made it possible for
him to use them with effect. He has, for instance, a trick of
doubling words; open anywhere and you find phrases like

this—'Gratian *loved* and *revered* him as a father'—or—'*The relaxation of discipline* and the *disuse of exercise* rendered the soldiers *less able* and *less willing* to support the fatigues of the service'.

This is not done merely to add a spurious weightiness to simple statements. It is done, almost always, with the express purpose of slowing down the narrative at those points on which Gibbon wants the reader's mind to dwell. He thus detains the reader's attention by the simple device of making him read more slowly. But he never exactly duplicates his phrases; the additions are artistically correct, because they add to or modify the meaning. In the hands of less skilful writers, who duplicated without art and without apparent reason, the trick which was widely copied became intolerable.

The chance by which the *Decline and Fall* came to be written looks almost providential; here was an English mind with the romantic bent of the English—evident in his early reading and tastes—carefully cultivated in the French tradition and saturated with French culture. He produced in consequence, in the most exact and expressive English, a history which is a model of lucid exposition and balanced form yet which never loses that undercurrent of feeling essential to great historical writing.

The *Decline and Fall of the Roman Empire* is an outstanding work of English scholarship and one of the great monuments of English eighteenth-century literature. This double achievement has had a profound influence on the whole tradition of English historical writing. The increasing complexity of techniques of historical research, and the ever more exacting standards of scholarly accuracy which began to prevail in the later nineteenth century, thanks to the massive and precise scholarship of the Germans, inevitably divorced history from literature. But in England this divorce never became complete and the re-union of history and literature in this country in our own time, may be traced in part to the influence of Gibbon. His method and manner and his splendid assurance may no longer be the models by which modern English historians work but he remains the presiding genius of our historical literature. The union of erudition and style which he achieved is still the ideal of the English tradition.

EDWARD GIBBON

A Select Bibliography

(Place of publication London, unless stated otherwise)

Bibliography, etc.

A BIBLIOGRAPHY OF THE WORKS . . . , by J. E. Norton (1940).
A critical bibliography of outstanding quality and interest.

THE LIBRARY OF EDWARD GIBBON, edited by G. L. Keynes (1940).
An annotated catalogue of Gibbon's books.

Separate Works:

ESSAI SUR L'ETUDE DE LA LITTERATURE (1761). *Criticism.*
A hack translation of Gibbon's French original appeared in 1764.

MEMOIRES LITTERAIRES DE LA GRANDE BRETAGNE (1768 and 1769). *Review.*
Produced by Gibbon and Deyverdun, the two annual volumes of
this unsuccessful literary review contain a number of anonymous
contributions by Gibbon.

CRITICAL OBSERVATIONS ON THE SIXTH BOOK OF THE AENEID (1770).
Criticism.
Published anonymously.

THE DECLINE AND FALL OF THE ROMAN EMPIRE, 6 vols. 4to (1776–88).
12 vols. 8vo (1783–90). *History.*
An edition with critical apparatus, edited by J. B. Bury, 7 vols.
1896–1900; and a 7 vol. edition with bibliography by H. M. Beatty
1909–14 are of great value. Popular reprints include the World's
Classics, 7 vols. and Everyman's Library, 6 vols.

A VINDICATION OF SOME PASSAGES IN THE FIFTEENTH AND SIXTEENTH
CHAPTERS OF THE HISTORY OF THE DECLINE AND FALL . . . (1779).
Commentary.

MEMOIRE JUSTIFICATIF &c (1779). *Politics.*
Written (anonymously) on the instructions of the Government.

MISCELLANEOUS WORKS . . . WITH MEMOIRS OF HIS LIFE AND WRITINGS
COMPOSED BY HIMSELF, edited by Lord Sheffield. 2 vols. 4to (1796).
5 vols. 8vo (1814).
A third 4to volume was added in 1815 to complete Lord Sheffield's
edition of 1796, with the additional material in the 1814 edition.

THE AUTOBIOGRAPHIES OF EDWARD GIBBON . . . , edited by J. Murray (1896).
The memoirs edited separately from the manuscripts used by Lord Sheffield for his 1796 edition of the Miscellaneous Works.

THE MEMOIRS OF THE LIFE OF EDWARD GIBBON . . . , edited by G. Birkbeck Hill (1900).
An edition with full critical apparatus. The editions of J. B. Bury (World's Classics, 1907) and O. Smeaton (Everyman's Library, 1911), both several times reprinted, should be noted.

Letters and Journals:

PRIVATE LETTERS OF EDWARD GIBBON, 1753–1794, edited by R. E. Prothero. 2 vols. (1896).

LA VIE DE SOCIETE DANS LE PAYS DE VAUD A LA FIN DU 18e SIECLE, par M. et Mme. W. de Savery. 2 vols. Lausanne (1911–12).
The primary source for Gibbon's later years at Lausanne.

GIBBON'S JOURNAL TO JANUARY 28TH 1763. MY JOURNAL AND EPHEME-RIDES I, II AND III, edited by D. M. Low (1929).

THE LETTERS OF EDWARD GIBBON, edited by J. E. Norton. 3 vols. (1955).
The definitive edition.

Some Biographical and Critical Works:

ESTIMATES OF SOME ENGLISHMEN AND SCOTCHMEN, by W. Bagehot (1858).
Includes a study of Gibbon.

GIBBON, by J. C. Morrison (1878).
In the English Men of Letters Series.

PROCEEDINGS OF THE GIBBON COMMEMORATION, 1794–1894. Royal Historical Society (1895).
Includes a catalogue of an exhibition at the British Museum of MSS., notebooks, portraits, etc.

SOME OXFORD THINKERS, by A. Cecil (1909).

GIBBON AND CHRISTIANITY, by E. Clodd (1916).

GIBBON, by J. M. Robertson (1925).

PORTRAITS IN MINATURE, by L. Strachey (1931).
Includes a study of Gibbon.

GIBBON, by G. M. Young (1932).
A brilliant essay.

GIBBON'S ANTAGONISM TO CHRISTIANITY, by S. T. McCloy (1933).
Contains a full list of the numerous contemporary works attacking
Gibbon.

EDWARD GIBBON, by C. Dawson (1934).
A lecture at the British Academy.

EDWARD GIBBON AND HIS AGE, by E. Blunden, Bristol (1935).
A lecture at Bristol University.

EDWARD GIBBON, by D. M. Low (1937).
The standard biography, admirable in every respect.

FOUR PORTRAITS, by Peter Quennell (1945).
Includes a study of Gibbon.

EDWARD GIBBON, by M. Joyce (1953).
In the 'Men and Books' Series.

EDWARD GIBBON E LA CULTURA EUROPEA DEL SETTECENTO, per G.
Giarrizzo, Naples (1954).